First Facts® PREDATOR PROFILES

LIONS
– BUILT FOR THE HUNT –

by Tammy Gagne

Consultant: Dr. Jackie Gai, DVM
Wildlife Veterinarian

CAPSTONE PRESS
a capstone imprint

First Facts are published by Capstone Press,
1710 Roe Crest Drive, North Mankato, Minnesota 56003
www.mycapstone.com

Library of Congress Cataloging-in-Publication Data
Gagne, Tammy, author.
  Lions : built for the hunt / by Tammy Gagne.
    pages cm.—(First facts. Predator profiles)
  Audience: Ages 6-9.
  Audience: K to grade 3.
  Summary: "Describes the features, behaviors, and adaptations that make lions skilled
predators"—Provided by publisher.
  Includes bibliographical references and index.
  ISBN 978-1-4914-8260-5 (library binding)
  ISBN 978-1-4914-8262-9 (eBook PDF)
  1. Lion—Juvenile literature. 2. Predation (Biology)—Juvenile literature. I. Title.
QL737.C23G347 2016
599.757—dc23   2015020222

Editorial Credits
Carrie Braulick Sheely, editor; Sarah Bennett and Juliette Peters, designers;
Tracy Cummins, media researcher; Tori Abraham, production specialist

Photo Credits
Getty Images: Michael Fairchild, 18-19; iStockphoto: 2630ben, 15; Shutterstock: Anna
Omelchenko, Cover, bjogroet, 6, creativex, 13, ivanmateev, 17, J Reineke, 10, Johan
Swanepoel, 1, john michael evan potter, 21, Ludmila Yilmaz, 20, luyao, 7, Maggy Meyer, 8-9,
Mogens Trolle, 5, paula french, Cover Back, Stephanie Periquet, 2, 3, 11, Tony Brindley, 16

Printed and bound in China.

007479LEOS16

TABLE OF CONTENTS

THE HUNTER AND THE HUNTED

Eight lions stand quietly in the grass watching a zebra. While grazing the zebra has slowly moved away from its **herd**. The zebra outweighs the lions. But it is going to have a tough time winning a fight against these powerful **predators**. The zebra's only hope will be outrunning the large cats.

Almost all lions live in Africa. A small number also live in India. Lions are among Africa's top predators. Their strength and **stealth** make them skillful hunters.

FACT
The lion's position as a top predator earns it the nickname "king of the beasts."

herd—a large group of animals that lives or moves together

predator—an animal that hunts other animals for food

stealth—having the ability to move secretly

4

BRINGING HOME DINNER

Lions live in groups called prides. Each pride is made up of about 15 lions. Usually only two or three of these lions are males. In many other animal **species**, the males are the hunters. But female lions feed a pride. They do nearly all the hunting.

FACT

Even though the females catch the food, the males are the first to eat it. The other lions then fight for their share of the food.

species—a group of animals with similar features

BIG, STRONG, AND FAST

A lion's size, speed, and strength are all helpful for hunting. Female lions weigh between 200 and 300 pounds (91 and 136 kilograms). Males can weigh up to 550 pounds (250 kg). Lions can run at speeds up to 50 miles (80 km) per hour. Muscular bodies help lions take down animals weighing up to 1,000 pounds (454 kg).

FACT

When they have gone a long time without eating, some lions will attack elephants. An adult elephant can weigh 25 times more than a lion!

DON'T MAKE A SOUND!

Female lions hunt in groups. Each one approaches the **prey** from a different direction. As they **stalk** the prey, the lions seem to know that movement creates sound. They move as slowly as possible. When sneaking through grass, some lions even turn their paws sideways, which makes less noise.

FACT

Lions' bodies seem made for stalking. Their paws have large, soft pads that help them walk quietly.

prey—an animal hunted by another animal for food

stalk—to hunt slowly and quietly

READY, SET ... POUNCE!

When they're close enough to prey, lions **pounce**. Once they catch their prey, lions use their powerful jaws and sharp teeth to kill it. Sometimes they break the animal's neck in one bite, killing it instantly. Other times they use their jaws to squeeze the animal's throat until it stops breathing.

FACT

Lions can leap as far as 36 feet (11 meters). That is about the length of three hippos!

pounce—to jump on something suddenly and grab it

NIGHTTIME HUNTERS

Lions are most active at night. With less light, it's harder for prey to see the lions coming. The lions' coloring also helps them hide. The coloring blends in with tall grass and other surroundings. Like other big cats, lions have **sensitive** hearing and can see well in the dark.

Lions also have an excellent sense of smell. A lion's nose helps it locate prey as well as the kills of nearby predators. Lions sometimes steal food from other animals.

FACT

Lions can see about six times better at night than during the day. Their **pupils** become bigger at night to let in more light.

sensitive—able to feel or react to things easily
pupil—the opening in the iris that controls the amount of light entering the eye

A HEALTHY APPETITE

When prey is limited, lions can go more than a week without eating. But they make up for the lack of food later. A hungry male lion can eat 83 pounds (38 kg) of meat in one day.

FACT

In the 1940s more than 450,000 lions lived in Africa. Today only about 25,000 are found in the wild. People have caused this decline by hunting lions and taking over their land.

POWERFUL PROTECTORS

As female lions hunt, the males usually rest—unless they sense another predator nearby. The males protect the pride's hunting territory. Adult males chase away other predators such as hyenas. A male lion's mane protects it during fights.

FACT

A male that joins a new pride will kill all the existing cubs. The male does this to remove his competition for head of the pride.

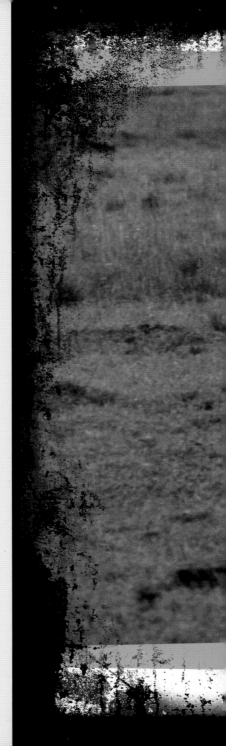

HUNTING LESSONS

Female lions give birth to between one and four cubs at a time. When the cubs are about nine months old, the females start taking them hunting. The cubs watch carefully as the adults stalk prey. The cubs copy this behavior. Soon they will be hunting on their own as powerful predators.

FACT

Lions let cubs practice hunting prey the adults have already injured. Cubs also pretend to fight with one another to practice hunting.

AMAZING BUT TRUE!

Both male and female lions roar loudly. Sometimes they roar to let other lions know they are nearby. Other times lions roar to claim territory. They also make this deep noise to scare away other animals. The sound is as loud as live rock music. An adult lion's roar can be heard from up to 5 miles (8 km) away!

GLOSSARY

herd (HURD)—a large group of animals that lives or moves together

pounce (POUNSS)—to jump on something suddenly and grab it

predator (PRED-uh-ter)—an animal that hunts other animals for food

prey (PRAY)—an animal hunted by another animal for food

pupil (PYU-pil)—the opening in the iris that controls the amount of light entering the eye

sensitive (SEN-si-tiv)—able to feel or react to things easily

species (SPEE-sheez)—a group of animals with similar features

stalk (STAWK)—to hunt slowly and quietly

stealth (STELTH)—having the ability to move secretly

territory (TER-uh-tor-ee)—an area of land that an animal claims as its own to live in

READ MORE

Marsh, Laura. *Lions.* National Geographic Kids. Washington, D.C.: National Geographic, 2015.

Ritchey, Kate. *Lion, Tiger, and Bear.* New York: Penguin Young Readers, 2014.

Throp, Claire. *Lions.* Living in the Wild: Big Cats. Chicago: Heinemann Library, 2014.

INTERNET SITES

FactHound offers a safe, fun way to find Internet sites related to this book. All of the sites on FactHound have been researched by our staff.

Here's all you do:

Visit *www.facthound.com*

Type in this code: 9781491482605

Check out projects, games and lots more at
www.capstonekids.com

CRITICAL THINKING
USING THE COMMON CORE

1. Name a feature that helps lions be stealthy. Explain how this feature helps lions sneak up on prey. (Key Ideas and Details)

2. The population of lions in Africa has been declining for years. What will happen if all lions die out? Explain an action people can take to help lion populations increase. (Integration of Knowledge and Ideas)

INDEX